View from the Middle of the Road V

New Observations

I0547212

Poems and Short Stories

Lucinda Clark
R. Xavier Clark
Silvana Marconi

PUBLISHING

Martinez, Georgia

P.R.A. Publishing
P.O. Box 211701
Martinez, Georgia 30917
www.prapublishing.com

ISBN: 9781941416-14-3 paperback
ISBN: 9781941416-15-0 electronic book
LCCN: 2018935983

Published in the United States of America

I Survived Silvana Marconi

Dedication

Women all over the world
united in what they see.
The world is changing
not just geographically
our truths are shared
our beliefs are aired
No longer are we scared.

We are women.
Hear us purr
see us unite
see us speak with one voice.
Now
Hear us roar!

For all the girls (soon-to-be women) of the world!

Lucinda J. Clark

Table of Contents

Mantra of a Bridge Builder

I am a bridge builder.
I build based upon where
I travel.

I build on happy days and sad days:
I have built during times I felt I could not—
and possibly should not—go on.

My bridge building is based on
following a road;
a dominant thought
changes in my world view.

Added to each bridge structure are
things I have seen,
things I have heard,
things I have read.
Ideas I have opened and closed
my eyes, heart, and mind to.

The length and strength of some of these bridges are
undetermined and
much too far away
for my mind's eye to reach;
only the passage of time
will determine.

Each bridge's purpose is to open new
gateways,
passageways,
and give opportunity
to those who are and are not like me.

To enrich all just by having come this way.

Maybe,
just maybe,
when my bridge building days are done,
what has been built
(even as I lapse into dust)
lives on.

Four Roads

Four roads diverged into a yellow wood.
Sorry I could not travel all
and still be one traveler.
Long I stood
and looked at all as long as I could.

Several years later all still equally stood
trenched deep with many a
success and failure of effort.

Four roads diverged and
I had taken them all.
It is only now that I
can see the difference.

Because

I get to the wood and find things changed;
I do not judge it as good or bad,
so changed am I from my journey,
for it is the realization
that, at some point,
I had taken all four roads.
I was never one traveler
but four rolled up
to look like one.

911 Update

We awoke on 9/11/01 to
planes crashing into the Twin Towers
acts of heroic bravery in our skies and
in our actions, with constant reminders on our TVs.
Prayers and memorials for all those who lost loved ones;
hatred for those who despise our way of life;
curiosity as to why we are so hated;
suggestions that we go shopping to prove
we have not been demoralized.

Reality Check 2017
In the time that has passed since that day
fights over how we should rebuild the towers
wars with enemies, proven and theoretical.
Elections of historical proportion
collapse of financial and social institutions
fear for our very way of life
Near collapse again of our institutions.
Prosperity for only those who—
violent outburst of intolerance
Anger, distrust, contempt for those who took an oath
to look after and protect our interests.
On social media there are
pleads to "fanatics" to "save" us.
We announce proudly to the world
that we too are killers.

How much progress have we made?
It now looks like our enemies
could have just waited it out
because we now destroy ourselves from within.
And this time, we can't go shopping to fix it;
it has all been spent on our way to today.

Chances Are

Is it a gift that once given cannot be taken back?
Or is it an opportunity?

I believe
A chance is an opportunity.
The goal, a lesson.

For a person who gives something
Someone a chance
Is learning to trust.
The receiver is learning humility.

Outcome

The giver learns if the gift was accepted as intended;
The receiver must show that it was.

Why?

Chances, like gifts,
May come once in a lifetime
For both giver and receiver.

At the end as in the beginning,
Expectations are everything.

Thinking of Spring

I remember your
readings
poems
willingness to serve
never pushy always kind

Sitting, standing, staring

There

waiting
wondering
wishing

For a chance, your chance

To

Stand up
Speak out
Scream
To Be Heard

I wanted so much for you:

The chance,
opportunity,
that moment,

To see it through;
see it happen;
to know
you mattered.

For Mahogany Red, RIP, January 2012.

A Mother's Love

A mother's love is
about holding on and letting go.

Holding on to the belief
that what you see the first time
you look into the eyes of your child
is the light of her true potential

Holding on to the fact
that your striving to be
the best servant
while still being true to yourself
will be passed on and manifest
as your child's potential develops

Holding on is

holding your breath
and your tongue
as your child takes on many firsts:
days of school
dates and steps
across auditorium stages
in the first of many school graduations
off into adulthood
out into life

A mother's love knows
it is time to let go of worry
as she drives off
for the first time and every time
she gets behind the wheel of her car
on an airplane to go miles
and time zones away from you.

Letting go of can she afford it?
when she offers to take you out
for a meal,
a shopping trip,
a play date.
Ah, the letting go!
It stabs like a knife in the heart
if done wrong
but feels like a boulder sliding
off your shoulders if done right

There is no argument,
battle of wills,
no battling at all:
just a mother's knowing
that acknowledgment
by the tip of the head
hug or offer to help without asking

There is gratitude, love, and mutual respect

That what you, the mother, have
hoped
prayed
worked for,
with God's help
you now see manifested.

Jeska and Harry

Deciding she would be born a lively, liberated Libra
instead of a hard-charging Capricorn,

I should have known
this would be a sign of things to come.

At twenty-eight weeks
she moved from the center of the NICU
to the outer wall,

Deciding she was ready to come home.
Before I got retrenched at work,
she decided
my last day on my first day back
would be my exit from "traditional."

There was the usual throng of helpers
bringing food, diapers, and support.

It was not until they all left
we were alone
that our eyes met
in that moment

I knew
she was destined to be
the lightning rod for inspiration,
not just for herself, but for us all.

She wanted a dog.

Not the cute little fluff balls of fur
yelping excitedly, grateful
for our attention.

She selected a little terrier,
shivering quietly in the corner of his cage.

Despite my protest,
we take him home.

She named him Harry;
I called him
      Sun Dog
       Earth Dog
        Protector Dog
         Adventure Dog
          Harry Houdini.

Eighteen years later,
we call him the old man and her young woman.

Momma II—It's Harry

I wanted you to know I always knew
From the first day I
Laid eyes on you with Momma JCC
We were gonna be something special.

The ladies from the shelter told you my name was Henry.
I was a skinny thing set way back in the corner of my cage
With all the happy, friendly dogs yapping for your favor.
You were kind enough to let Momma JCC bring me home,
Even though your eyes kept wandering over
To what you thought would be a better choice;
You trusted Momma JCC's instincts:
Thanks for that.

When Momma JCC taught me
How to open all the doors
And escape on adventures,
I knew you were just pretending to be mad.

To make sure I learned all those tricks you taught me,
I think that helped you overlook
My "self-walks."

Well, eventually,
I appreciate the heart-to-hearts we had
As Momma and Papa X prepared to go off to college.
Sorry for tearing things up;
I was mad, especially when you told me I could not go to Arizona
And sleeping in bed with you was never gonna happen.
Thank Mishcu for helping me with that.

We grew closer:
If you don't believe me,
Check out the family pics.
You always let me know when Momma was coming home and
Showed me places on the map as she became a world traveler.

Tell Daddy Man and Papa X
I always appreciated the cheese treats and walks
And the encouragement to run free.

Thanks for stepping up
When you knew it was time for me to finally go
And allowing me to go with dignity.
I'm doing the sit, down, and roll over like in the old days—
Pain-free!

Thanks for the love.
Don't miss me
'Cause we dwell in each other's hearts
I think you call it memories.

When you think of me now,
Know I'm off on my biggest, best adventure.
Bye.

Alien Observation I—Lipstick

Some would say for women it is an essential
no self-respecting lady would
be caught dead without.

The multicolored cylinder is deceptive
for what lies within has much significance, my friend.
It has the power to transform a tight-laced soul into a harlot—
a plain-Jane's features come to life with just two strokes.

Oh, yes,
that small compact cylinder
sitting harmlessly there
contains a substance that
has seen many a military man off to war,
stained many coffee cups,
sealed many love letters,
even tucked small children into bed at night.

It has smudged many a cheek in friendship
and served as proof of infidelity.

It has covered lips
that have cried out over injustices,
marked many things as a sign of love.

That cylinder contains
what they call "lipstick,"
comes in more colors and shades
then you can imagine.

Its powers are intensified
by the woman who puts it on,
for it is rare
for the males of the species to indulge.

Understand its true purpose:
to enhance the inner beauty
that she,
the wearer,
already possesses inside.

Alien Observation II—Golf

Want to share with you what I learned about a game.
No, that's not right, a sport
that is very popular
amongst a certain set.
I may have misidentified it
because depending on whom you believe

It's described as
a game,
a sport,
like religion,
and a weekend widow maker.

It involves things like
bunkers, greens, and fairways,
tees and sand traps,
carts and foursomes,
drivers, irons, putters,
and a tiny white ball.

It ends after 18 holes
with par 3s, par 5s,
and lots of water.

That little ball is
chipped, birded, bogged, driven,
and holed in one; this last one gets a player very excited!

It's played in
country clubs,
on beaches,
on recycled landfills,
in swamplike areas with alligators,
and in beautiful places like Augusta.

I was told that, at one time, only rich guys played.
Now, all kinds of guys do,
and lots of women, too.
Even children play.

It has heroes and legends and chokers
like
Arnie, Jack, and Tiger—
and one called "Greg the Shark."

At first, I thought it was all about striking a tiny white ball many times over
great and small distances for hours.

Then, I went out to where they play and learned
it's a solo player with a bag of clubs and a tiny white ball,
out in jaw-droppingly beautiful natural settings,
battling to be his best self.

Sergio Garcia and the Golf Gods

He strolls up to the fifteenth hole,
Seventy-four tries at being first in his head
Seventy-four failures to snatch the prize

He calls on his golf ancestors
To step in and intercede on his behalf
Just once on this special day

Because the vengeful Golf Gods had gathered.
They were there determined to make it failure seventy-five.
Their intent to succeed again at the Masters
In putting Sergio's face in the dust of defeat

This time they failed.

To Rock the Mic Again

It is good to know
your days of rockin' the mic
will never be behind you.

That even as you find yourself passing
your years in a nursing home,
you can give joy, hope,
and inspiration by rocking
your favorite poetry gem.

You felt the call to step up
even at ninety years old
'cause the soul of a poet
never leaves this earth as long as
her words are down on paper,
and she shares them.

With all they were worth,
when you set them aside
to hold down that job
and take care of the future,
you thought as a poet and held on tight;
you got a chance to rock the mic again.

Dedicated to Myrtle Miller, Washington Commons, Augusta, Ga. April 27,
2016

A Tanda to Remember

You took me away
on the hard wooden dance floor
by the power of your soulful, melodic lead.

Song one:
Your embrace leads me to step gracefully,
carefully as we learn at what level we would engage.

Song two:
I *ocho cortado* backward and forward
your lead that is now balanced and smooth.

By *Song Three:*
Your lead confident,
our movements are now rhythmic and fluid:
as the sultry accordion keeps time in the background,
exhausted from the exhilaration of the set
we leave the dance floor, all smiles and glowing
sure that this was a tanda to remember.

Tanda: set of three to four songs played during a milonga.

Black People Don't Tango

R. Xavier Clark

As I watched them glide gracefully across the room, I was completely entranced. A smooth, pulsing rhythm of an accordion filled my being. The dim, red lighting of the small theater felt spacious, yet very intimate. The sultry delicacy of each move was calculated to the micrometer; oh, the harmony! The scene was magnetic.

Even in Buenos Aires, the art of tango had not lost its potent aura. The crowd was just as enthralled as I was, and as I glanced out of the corner of my eye, I realized that everyone's mouth was shaped to make their amusement as clear as glass. A beautiful, tan woman in an orange gown three tables away stroked her lips slowly, in sync with the dancers. A Latin man standing in the corner, wearing a white tuxedo and smoking a cigar, shook his head in disbelief—ever so fierce, yet ever so smooth.

The first act was but an appetizer for what was to come. As the show persisted and came to life, each number brought a new barrage of dazzling choreography, executed by some of the most gorgeous and lively people I had ever seen, all bending the laws of what seemed possible.

I knew that behind the scenes were hours and hours of hot, sweat-filled practice, carried out over years of study. I knew that dance masters were capable of a level of perfectionism so acute that even a valedictorian from Juilliard would break down into tears. Pain. Struggle. Blood. I knew this because my parents had studied the art of tango for almost two years now.

Of course, my father never wanted to dance. A strong and proud man, I was surprised to learn that he felt tense and uneasy at the very thought of dancing. My mother had tried in vain for decades to convince him that dancing would be fun for both of them.

"I don't want to," said my father, in a very matter-of-fact tone.

"You would be good; you have a great sense of rhythm!" exclaimed my mother in a futile attempt to persuade an unpersuadable man.

"No."

This exact conversation was cycled over and over, about every 4 years or so, with the same result, time after time. Eventually, my mother had the clever idea to give my father a coupon for five tango lessons as a Christmas present.

They expired unused.

After another three years, she was finally able to drag my father into the local studio against his will, in a way that only a wife, or mother, could do. The teacher was a young woman with blond hair and a shirt that looked like it was made entirely of glitter and happy thoughts.

"You two look like such a happy couple! I can't wait to get you guys into our upcoming amateur show!"

God bless my father; it must have taken every ounce of restraint in his possession to avoid running straight out of the studio, hopping into the car, turning onto the interstate, and fleeing to Mexico. He is certainly a better man than I.

Lo and behold, after the first five lessons, my father agreed to schedule another five sessions, and then another five after that. After fifteen lessons, he actually began to enjoy the challenge. He began to appreciate the subtlety of the various techniques. He began to respect the amount of skill it took to memorize steps while keeping a strong frame and leading your partner. As a man of supreme discipline, he also began to respect the amount of work it took not only to become a professional, but even to become an above-average dancer.

Then came tragedy.

My father began to receive compliments on his dancing ability, and there was no turning back: The floodgates had opened. My mother was reasonably happy to have her husband transform into a dancing fiend . . . in the beginning. After a year of weekly lessons, my father began to improve exponentially. As his skills grew, so did his intensity.

"Honey, can you . . . What are you watching?"

Her husband was staring, transfixed at his laptop. She leaned in closer.

"I'm watching the World Tango Olympics. Juan De Campo Valdez and his partner Susie Legarza are amazing! They just did a combo boleo and then dissociated while . . ."

My mother was so horrified that she tuned out. For fifteen years, she had begged this man to dance, pleaded with him to amuse her with a couple's instruction. When she finally convinced, correction . . . *forced*, him to take lessons, she had gotten more than she had bargained for. A few days earlier, he had revealed that he was squeezing quick lessons into some of his lunch breaks. He had begun to order tango magazines. His ring tone was now "Milonga del Angel." To make things even more outrageous, an electronic billboard down the street from their house featured him promoting the dance studio with the owner. Seriously! To top it off, here he was watching the "World Tango Olympics," which she wasn't even familiar with, when he was supposed to be planning a trip for their anniversary. My mother didn't know whether to laugh or cry at the irony.

She decided to be angry.

"This has gotten to be too much!" she said abruptly.

As a man married for more than 25 years now, my father was accustomed to vague and seemingly random moments of emotion from his better half. Being the intelligent person he was, as well as a student of the human condition, he knew that his wife was unhappy about something; he wasn't sure about what, however.

"Too much? What has gotten to be too much?" He knew that during the summer months, the air-conditioning tended to elevate the electric bill. Perhaps this was making her unsure that they could afford the lavish trip to Saint Lucia they were planning for their anniversary. He luckily had run the numbers several times and was quite sure they could. He was mentally preparing the best way to present this information when my mother said:

"The dancing . . . You go to three lessons every week, and you want me to stop what I'm doing and come with you. Then, every weekend, you want to go to dance parties across the country so that we can tango in festivals, people's houses . . . I mean two weekends ago, we even tangoed on the beach!"

My father was surprised. He was a bit confused, also, because he wasn't sure which part of what she said was bad albeit completely true; they had recently returned from a weekend-long tango event, which, at one point, featured a transition from dancing on the beaches of Charleston, South Carolina, to a beachfront house party where the dancing continued. He did have three lessons per week and did extend the invitation every time. Being that everything my mother stated could be agreed to as being factual, he calculated that it was clear to speak his mind.

"Well . . ." He paused as he suddenly realized that he was actually walking a slippery slope, with starving alligators licking their chops should he lose his footing.

"Well . . . What's wrong with that?"

"Nothing . . . except for the fact that two of those three lessons are an hour away. Plus, I like to dance, not to practice dancing. Lessons can be so serious, and to be honest, sometimes it drains the fun out of the whole thing. I mean, dancing is supposed to be fun!"

"In about two more years, I will be right where I want to be skills-wise. Until then, I need to practice!"

Now, my mother had the luxury of being a fairly naturally skilled dancer and could only mildly appreciate the position my father was in and, interestingly enough, vice versa. My father could only mildly appreciate the position my mother was in but decided that, as usual, there was some basis about what she was saying.

"What do you think is the best thing to do then?" he asked.

My mother thought for a minute and said, "I'm going to take some time from going to the lessons, but I want you to keep going. When you're there, dance with as many different people as you can, and then you will get enough experience leading and . . ." she stopped for emphasis, "and learn not to step on your partner's feet."

As the show in Buenos Aires raged on, I took the last sip from my cocktail. I scanned the room again, saw our waitress, and flagged her down. When she arrived at our table, I placed an order for another of the same concoction. The night had just begun, and this show was fantastic, so I figured a second drink was in order.

The band had somehow moved from the stage area to behind the audience; however, the piano player remained on stage. As he hammered out note after note, the crowd whistled and cheered. The four dancers on stage spun and flipped, and the women wrapped their legs in gold medal Olympics-type contortions. I turned to my sister.

"You should put this in your documentary," I shouted toward her as the shimmer of one of the dancer's sequined outfits undoubtedly put a twinkle in my eye.

My older sister was something of a Renaissance woman, and at this point in her life, was shooting two separate documentaries: One was about climate change and the creation of the Great Garbage Patch off the coast of Patagonia; the other film was a time-capsule project in collaboration with one of Hollywood's hottest directors. Naturally, I was referring to the latter.

"That's a good idea, but I think that if I'm going to add any tango sequences, I would want them to be of Mom and Dad," she yelled over the music and crowd. I laughed as the waitress brought me my second drink.

"Everyone knows black people don't tango!"

After a few months of going to lessons without my mother, my father's skill did continue to improve. Dancing with new partners did allow him to learn how to lead and thus freed him to focus on his moves; his comfort level increased, as well. He participated in his second amateur show and received stellar feedback on his performance. Needless to say, I was quite proud of him.

During our trip in Buenos Aires, my sister managed to capture some footage of the two of them dancing at the hotel, which became a part of the time-capsule footage for her collaboration with the Hollywood director. Apparently, all people tango.

After a long day, I came home to our house to get ready for the weekend. It was not yet evening, but it was already starting to get dark. I gathered some things, mostly clothes, a toothbrush, deodorant, a towel, and some things I would need for a road trip to visit close friends for a few days. After loading my car, I went back inside to tell my parents good-bye and to let them know I would see them soon. It was later in the afternoon, and the house had most of the lights out, but there was a strip of light coming from underneath the door of my parents' bedroom. As I approached the door to knock, I suddenly heard the sound of my mother giggling, followed by a laugh from my father . . . followed by the sound of tango music.

Transition from How Things Used to Be

Transition
in politics,
description for tragedies
formatting for self-awareness exercises.

We are forced into transition
we move from complacency to activism,
in silent voices to angry ones shouting from the streets
our private belief turning to open declarations to God.

From secure to insecure,
fired up to numb

From bullied to confident;
in solitude
walled off within families and in public.

We pray and pray,
ask for prayers,
send out prayers,

Then declare only certain prayers
can, should, or will be answered;
the others' prayers not good enough to be counted.

We keep it real
then apologize or not

Scrolling social media,
condemning it at the same time,
feeling powerless or too powerful to stop
condemning as we type

We used to believe that being polite is correct
until we find it unnecessary as we strive
to get attention and hopefully
that which we believe we deserve.

Our parents taught us the importance
of expanding our world view
that to be different, independent
in our thinking and actions, was good.

Reaching out
globally,
peacefully,
to some yet-to-be
determined destination.

The Inner Voices Return

I toil in the realm of the invisible,

My voice

Strangled

Muted.

My options

Infinite
Limited

Never-endingly

upended

My choices:

Get Voice
Give Voice

Do it now!

For My Sisters II

To all my sisters, no matter your image,
No matter where you reside in these United States,
No matter where you work,
Pray,
Get your nails and hair done.

No matter who you are married to,
No matter who your ancestors may be or
Your children will become—

One hundred years ago
We shared something in common.
We had no political voice,
No right to vote.

Ninety-seven years ago
Women and men
Set aside that which they did not
Have in common to fight
For the right for all to vote.

Today, we share this right and,
Whether you choose to exercise it or not,
It was hard won for us.

For all who would take issue
With my excitement and pride,

I ask that you tell

Your aunts, daughters, mothers, sisters, coworkers,
Any other female except me
That Women's Equality Day is stupid,

For it matters to
Those of us who celebrate and exercise this right
The first woman who will someday become president
And
Most importantly to the people in lands
Where the right to vote is not possible.

A New Thought on Time

All things take time.
How long?
How much time?
Depends, time that it takes.
Young people push time—rush
Old people want time to slow down—preserve
Middle-Agers just want to keep up—balance.
Important things take time.
How much time?
Sometimes, a lifetime.

I Survived

Silvana Marconi

My name is Silvana. I am 40 years old and live in Montevideo, Uruguay, precisely in the Nuevo Paris neighborhood. I was born, grew up, and lived through my darkest and most wonderful moments here.

Nuevo Paris is a very poor neighborhood, but its solidarity taught me to love it as it is: an icon of the productivity of other decades, with its factories and tanneries now closed; the golden leaves of many trees still powerful, even though winters and autumn dishevel their old scalps; a nursery of squares where you can smell the simple joys of childhood.

I am convinced that even if I was offered a chance to live in a more high-class neighborhood such as Pocitos or Carrasco, I would not think twice: I was born a Nuevo Parisian, and here I'll stay.

I have been teaching since I was 17 years old. I also work as a secretary at a major law firm in the center of downtown Montevideo.

I have been married for five years. My husband is a military man; I met him on the Internet when he was on a mission in the Republic of Congo.

I have two teenage children: a girl who is twelve years old, and boy who is fourteen.

We love animals. We have four dogs, and we all live in peace—especially me, really far away from the hell that I went through fifteen years ago.

They say that when someone has descended and returned from hell, they are committed to fulfilling some kind of mission. My mission is to tell about my stay in that infernal place. It took me a long time to decide that it was time to make my mission come true. I did not dare show the scars of human brutality given to me by those who always beat me.

Surviving domestic violence means much more than just saving your skin and relative sanity. I knew it when the words of this book began to burn in me.

The burning started on the bus one afternoon as I returned from work. I started to think of many beaten women who were ridiculed, stabbed, and even set on fire—so many unprotected and forgotten girls.

I thought: I am alive, thank God. I am respected by my family; I am remembered by friends. I am capable of generating projects like this one. There is no place for fear when one has these gifts. Not yet convinced of my determination to persevere, the former victim in me whispered: "Will you dare to proclaim yourself as an author?

"Will someone be offended? What if he (my former husband) comes for revenge?"

"I do not care. I am strong now; I have a voice now; and I will make it through the silence of the cowards so that—Ricardo—knows that I, Silvana Marconi, am not deformed and worthless. I am a source of light. My heart is filled with courage.

The First Date

As a child, I dreamed of starting a family. Obviously, for me, that meant getting married and having children, especially a boy. In high school, I loved to go dancing, although I always had problems, caused, in general, by my selfishness: my friends loved Cumbia, and I, Madonna. I had been a fan of the Brazilian singer Xuxa. I spent entire afternoons with my friends, pretending to be *paquitas* (paquitas were the dancers of Xuxa). I've been dazzled by Axl Rose's legs when he moved them to the rhythm of "Don't Cry." I even wore his bandanna. I preferred the comfort of jeans and sneakers; current fashion did not consume me.

At the age of twenty one, I ended a long-term relationship. I would accompany my mother on her rounds of shopping. She frequented a busy fruit and vegetable stand where everyone in the community bought from. A man and his mother were the owners. The man was tall with light brown hair and eyes. I thought that only clear eyes made a soul transparent, so I was struck by how his eyes captivated me; his gaze reminded me of a helpless child, and he had the blackest nails I had ever seen.

I did not hold back from asking a neighbor about him. She found out what she could. He was 24 years old, he did not have a girlfriend, he liked being with his family, and, above all, he did not smoke. My mother warned me not to take an interest in a man with dirty nails.

Saturday night, March 20, 1999, was our first date. My neighbor and others secretly waited for him to appear. I was in the corner, and I knew that he would arrive in his truck. We traveled all over Montevideo, from La Barra de Santa Lucía to Parque Rodó.

"Are you hungry?" he asked me suddenly. "Tell me, and I will go to the store to get some bananas."

The Relationship

We kept going out on Saturdays staying out until dawn; on weekdays, we saw each other for a little while at night or we talked for hours on the phone.

After a few months, things changed: He started dropping me at home at midnight. It really did not make me happy to see him for such a short time, but he said he had to go to bed early because he was tired from the drudgery of work that week. I did not argue with him; I tried to understand and not to be recriminatory.

The Engagement

After two years of the relationship, we decided to get engaged and bought the rings. My family knew, but Richardo did not dare inform his—more precisely—mother. Richardo's mother was a short, chubby, woman with very little hair, and face so pleasing that no one would suspect a hint of evil—a woman raised in the countryside stultified by work in the field during her adolescence. It was so hard for her son to face any issue with his mother that he begged me to say that I paid for the gold rings with my credit card. That seemed weird to me, but I didn't question his motives. (That's how brave my fiancé was, and how blind I was!) Anyway, his mother was angry because we had not shared with her in advance such an important event.

Maybe the ring request prodded my intuition. The next Saturday, after he left me at my parents' house at midnight, about fifteen minutes after his departure, it occurred to me to make a romantic call to him, but his mother answered the phone and said that he was not at home.

I did not think of him in an accident. My body froze instantly; my world fell apart.

I went out to step on the ruins. I ran, and I ran. I wanted to check that the truck was not stopped in front of his house; in fact, the truck was not there. I thought to myself:

Where is he?
Is he with another girl?
Is he dancing in some dirty place?
Are you faithful?
Where are you?

Why is my love not enough, my dedication, my understanding? Don't you realize I'm not fat? I cycle and hike. I care for my hair and curls, the face . . .

In that moment, I realized I'd begun to doubt him, and this was not the first time. It had started some time ago.

Out in the ruins, for two hours, I repeated these concerns as if he was in front of me—until he appeared. He was putting a ring on my finger. A few days later, I forgave him. Oh God, now I wonder why! There were too many signs not to realize that a time of pain was very close, but we women believe that our love is omnipotent.

Ruins (from the Latin *Ruina*) are the remains of human-made architecture: structures that were once intact have fallen, as time went by, into a state of partial or total disrepair, due to lack of maintenance or deliberate acts of destruction.

Excerpt taken from *Sobrevivi* by Silvana Marconi, published by Viking Libros, ISBN 978-9974-91767-5 @2018. Edited by L. J. Clark.

Other titles in the *View from the Middle of the Road* series

View from the Middle of the Road—Where the Greenest Grass Grows: ISBN 978097277031-6

View from the Middle of the Road II—U.S. in US: ISBN 978097277036-1

View from the Middle of the Road III—Quest for Knowledge: ISBN 978097277039-2

View from the Middle of the Road IV—Pathway to Dreams: ISBN 97898214070-3

View from the Middle of the Road V—New Observations: ISBN 978194141614-3